At The End of Masculine Time

A Case for Cultural Resistance

Dustcover

At **The End of Masculine Time** makes the case that modern liberal society is a Faustian matrix whereby the collective and individual souls of men are incinerated on The Altar, of what the author names 'the God of Things'.

This apostolic manifesto makes the case against the ever pervasive violence of civilization in favor of the serenity of barbarity.

This counter culture mediation on being a man in an emasculated society names the cause, enumerates the symptoms, and offers a cure for what ails men.

Includes the essays:
Echoes of Men
What Smokes on God's Altar
Superman and the Plight of Orks
Let the Weak Fall
In The Onion Field of the Soul
and, **Where Life is Scarce**

Key Words: masculinity, manhood, modernity

At the End of Masculine Time

Books by James LaFond

Nonfiction

The Fighting Edge, 2000
The Logic of Steel, 2001
The First Boxers, 2011
The Gods of Boxing, 2011
All Power Fighting, 2011
When You're Food, 2011
The Lesser Angles of Our Nature, 2012
The Logic of Force, 2012
The Greatest Boxer, 2012
Take Me to Your Breeder, 2014
The Streets Have Eyes, 2014
Panhandler Nation, 2014
The Ghetto Grocer, 2014
American Fist, 2014
Don't Get Boned, 2014
Alienation Nation, 2014
In The Chinks of The Machine, 2014
How the Ghetto Got My Soul, 2014
Saving the World Sucks, 2014
Taboo You, 2014
The Fighting Life, 2014
Narco Night Train, 2014
Into the Mountains of Madness: in [3 volumes], 2014
Incubus of Your Sacred Emasculation, 2014
Breeder's Digest, 2014
The Third Eye, 2015
Modern Agonistics, 2015
By the Wine Dark Sea, 2015
The Pale Usher, 2015
The Third Eye, 2015

Fiction

Astride the Chariot of Night, 2014
Sacrifix, 2014
Rise, 2014
Motherworld, 2014
Planet Buzzkill, 2014
Fruit of The Deceiver, 2014
Forty Hands of Night, 2014
Black and Pale, 2014
Daughters of Moros, 2014
Darkly, 2014
Fat Girl, 2015
Hurt Stoker, 2015
Poet, 2015
Triumph, 2015
Winter, 2015
The Spiral Case, 2015
Hemavore, with Dominick Mattero, 2015
Yusuf of the Dusk, 2015
Mantid, 2015
RetroGenesis: Day 1, with Erique Watson, 2015

Sunset Saga Novels

Big Water Blood Song, 2011
Ghosts of the Sunset World, 2011
Beyond the Ember Star, 2012
Comes the Six Winter Night, 2012
Thunder-Boy, 2012
The World is Our Widow, 2013
Behind the Sunset Veil, 2013
Den of The Ender, 2013
God's Picture Maker, 2014
Out of Time, 2015
Seven Moons Deep, 2015

At the End of Masculine Time

For Mescaline Franklin, my brother in Hate, may you bury your righteous blade in this rotten carcass we were born into

Contents

At the End of Masculine Time

If you flatter yourself that you are all over comfortable, and have been so a long time, then you cannot be said to be comfortable anymore."

-Herman Melville, Moby Dick

Echoes of Men: The Ghosts That Mould Us #1: Our Fathers

I was recently out drinking with a young fellow. We have in common the fact that we have often been attacked and threatened by black men and men of other colored ethnic groups. He is a self-described 'evil white racist.' But, he befriended a fellow black writer at the mixed-race sports bar, so I know better than to take him at his negative word concerning his prejudices. After all his antipathy of the darker races is based in experience, not theory, not blind hate, and is not prejudice at all.

The fellow I'm speaking of calls himself 'Mescaline' Franklin and is a refugee from Camden New Jersey, a place overrun by black crime in his lifetime. He now lives in a better part of the Garden State. He drove to Baltimore to acquire the publishing rights to one of my books ***An Arabian Terror Tale*** for his fledgling gonzo publishing empire **Forever Autumn Press** and paid for the rights by the pitcher at the mixed-race sports bar, and later by

9

the pint at the hipster micro-brew bar across the street.

As we spoke the barmaid—a pleasing example of Caucasian womanhood—overheard our science-fiction conversation and engaged us. As a writer who has travelled very little, when I meet such a person—who I think travelled extensively as a college student—my instinct is to ask about their travels, to try and imprint every word into my writer's mind.

I was beginning to hope 'Mescaline' and her would hit it off. Then she began relating a tale about her travels in Islamic Indonesia, where she often sallied forth alone without an itinerary, like some victim in a Criminal Minds episode, armed with nothing but her American status. Mescaline immediately became angry at the idea of a white woman socializing with another race of men. I felt the tension in his shoulder, saw his muscular jaw jut forward as he snarled about how our decadent liberal society had set her up and put her in danger and how lucky she had been to escape intact.

She was retrieving a beer from a cooler as her mouth formed an 'O' of surprise, her eyes bugged out worriedly, and her body began shelling up into a fetal position. He was actually scaring her. So I put a staying hand on his broad shoulder and linked her interrupted account of her meeting with a group of male Islamists around a campfire, just after they had received their AK-47s from recruiters. Indeed she had been difficult to pry into an admittance of such a thing as she had apparently been harassed by U.S. officials on her return from Indonesia concerning this girl's adventure of hers which had as its object nothing more than sightseeing around the isle of Flores. She was clearly an apolitical nerd of a cutie.

As I stayed him from his rant with a fatherly hand I encouraged her onward with her tale. "They treated you like a man didn't they?"

"Yes, they did. How did you know?"

"Since the 19th Century Western women have commonly received tacit recognition among primitives as occupying an extra-gender demigoddess stature. It will be changing. But you benefitted from a legacy of empire; of U.S. Marine and French Foreign Legion intervention around the world. The Western woman is still something of a cargo cult image in parts."

At the End of Masculine Time

The lady then continued with her tale—first mentioning cargo cult reverence demonstrated by these so called Islamists of a plane flying overhead—with a wary eye on Mescaline, as if he might be expected to turn into a werewolf.

As Mescaline and I walked home to the plantation house after closing the bar it occurred to me, that although our lives had been colored by very similar violent interracial experiences, we had had very different fathers. Our fathers are not the only men who influence us. Indeed I have often thought that some of my uncles were more influential than my father—perhaps because they were more fun, cooler, more outrageous, or more physical.

Consider the similarities in mine and Mescaline's relationships with our fathers. We were both estranged from our fathers at various times according to our own initiative—had both rejected our fathers. We now both live counter to the lessons taught by our fathers.

Mescaline's dad—a tough guy—advocated kicking ass, hunting and womanizing. Yet Mescaline is militantly celibate, involved in the technology field, and a very 'bohemian' writer.

At the End of Masculine Time

My father advocated success in business and devotion to the workplace, an avoidance of physical risk, and monogamous commitment to a stay-at-home wife. Yet I live as a loner, have turned my nose up at numerous high paying job offers, continue to compete in one of the most savage combat sports with men half my age, and remain a committed bachelor.

Mescaline and I live in a state of rejection of our fathers. Yet, when our buttons are pushed and our sensibilities disturbed, and even our lives threatened on the streets of our respective mid-sized American shit towns, we revert to our fathers' examples. Mescaline girds for combat with men, or bristles in preparation to scold an out of place woman after the manner of his street-fighting father, whereas I default to use of pacifying body language and behavioral manipulation, after the manner of my salesman/self-help counselor father, who believed—naïvely I think—in the manageability of any situation.

To me, in my mind, having just interviewed Mescaline about his upbringing in savage Camden, this said something about the imprint our fathers make on our subconscious minds, and also why those who have so often chosen me as an enemy—

and who so often grew to manhood in a fatherless state—seem to be making things up as they go along, with rarely a result in their favor.

Point of the Family Spear:
The Ghosts That Mould Us #2:
Uncles

In most primitive societies uncles are as important—and often more important—to the raising of a youth into a man as the father. For a little loner boy like me a get together with the extended family featured many positives and negatives. The big positive was listening to my uncles, the men, who at one time or another, I would wish I was as I stumbled along unsuccessfully as a wimpy alienated boy. By the time I had morphed into a savage feral youth I had internalized only a portion of what they taught me in an often unintentional way, as they conversed with each other.

Since many of us have been separated from our fathers and grandfathers by death or via the many methods our society uses to keep men out of the lives of their sons and grandsons, uncles can serve as very useful role models. My basic method when in the process of consciously assembling a behavioral arsenal that would help me survive the nocturnal streets of Baltimore in my late 20s and early 30s was to compare the behavior of one uncle with his results in the given situation I found myself in and then operate accordingly, adding anything useful I might have picked up along the way.

This article is partially meant as an ode to men who I have rarely recognized in writing, as well as an encouragement to younger men that they might have some relatives—often by marriage—with insights and experiences that might be useful to making your own way. Below are brief profiles of the uncles in my life and how they have helped me.

Uncle Fred: My Grandpa Kern's son and the most successful man in the extended family, Uncle Fred is a big alpha male. With the death of my father he stepped up to fill the void. He taught me how to network with men. He recently related a story about breaking man's leg in a 1950s college football game, and how he recently met with him at a conference in Florida or Texas without hard feelings.

Uncle Robert: Imagine Ralph Nadir as a mixed-race boxer who believed in UFO's nuking Sodom and Gomorrah. The family thought he was nuts but Robert was the smartest of us all and was way ahead of his time in many ways, predicting our current economic crisis for instance, back in the 1970s. Uncle Robert taught me the virtue of defiance and that it must be backed by investigation.

Uncle Bernie: My Aunt Ann's husband was a deer and bear hunter who liked shooting Chi-Coms in

North Korea even more. He was hit in the ass by a sub-machinegun round up near the Yalu River when the 8th Army was overrun. Bernie believed that belligerence was an important enough masculine quality to deserve to be effective, and that the best way to be an effective belligerent was to have the right tool, the right skill set for the tool, and the appropriate concept of its application. I could not watch a western with him—with my chin propped up by the skull of his bear skin rug—without him ranting and raving about horses not being shot to turn the 'goddamned redskins' into infantry. Also, as a racial motivated man who believed in making black men swim back to Africa with a Jew under one arm and an Italian under the other [which was quite a testament, I thought, as to Uncle Robert's athletic ability], he taught me that you could be against a group and still deal amicably with members of that group.

Uncle John: My father's older brother—who still roller blades and tango dances—taught the art of drawing a person into conversation as a way of building something together, rather than as a method of verbal sniping pr manipulation.

Uncle Herb: My Aunt Marie's second husband was the only member of my family that believed in me as a writer. He was an engineer on a merchant marine ship and kept a vast library which I freely borrowed from as a boy. In his opinion, "Nothing beats knowing what the hell some idiot did in the past, in hopes that you won't do it."

Uncle Bill: My Aunt Alice's husband was extremely quiet, wore a black suit and fedora, and used to sneak me beers at family functions when I was a little tyke. As his neighborhood was overrun by blacks and his sons fought in the streets and alleys he minded his own business, and even after his sons were grown or gone, still walked the streets unmolested. When my Grandma Kern found out that I was travelling in black areas at night and by bus she said, "Be like your Uncle Bill; nobody—and I mean nobody—has ever laid a hand on your Uncle Bill. He was a gentle man with my sister, but no man ever crossed him and was able to tell of it."

As I found myself increasingly in these men's shoes, I often took the simple course of asking myself, "What would Unk do?"

Where Life is Scarce: The Ghosts That Mould Us #3: Our Grandfathers

I knew very little about my father's father. I did know my mother's father, so it was he who I looked to as a living ancestor. He always had an ancestral feel about him. As a house painter in the 1930s he used to walk 20 to 40 miles per day, just to get back and forth to his work sites. Now when an American man does that it is a tragedy, it is international news! He taught me the value of walking, of separating from our means of transportation and seeing the world in a more intimate way. He was also quiet, reserved and measured, never ranting and raving like his wife, and never vexed by her antics.

My three strongest memories of Grandpa Kern are:
1. His talking to my brother and I about not enlisting for military service, that it was a devil's bargain that served some little understood and possibly unjust purpose.
2. His dropping me off 8 miles from the city line when I moved to Baltimore and telling me to walk down town and not turn back until I found a job.

19

3. Watching video of Egyptian President Anwar Sadat being killed at a parade review, and seeing the slow motion shot of a loyal officer running an assassin through with his ceremonial sword. Grandpa smiled and grinned at me, speaking approvingly of one man's ability to employ his character to take out a much better armed man, "That is the way. I bet he felt that!"

After Grandpa passed I thought he had just instructed me on 'keeping cool' as part of the process of dominating the women and networking with the men in your life without a fuss, and of the importance of hard work and independence; of knowing you can get to your job even if the busses are not running or your car is broken down. But I have come to realize what he was really teaching was an active Western way of meditation.

Since my teens I have had to listen to practitioners of Asian-based martial arts extol the virtues of everything Asian and the weakness of everything Western: such as boxers being unable to punch, wrestlers being unable to fight, and any 80 year old 100 pound karate master being able to disarm burly gunmen at will. Much of this has been said to stem from the meditative arts, to come from the strong spirit developed sitting in peaceful mind-emptying repose.

At the End of Masculine Time

The truth is boxers mediate when they shadowbox, wrestlers when they roll by themselves. The ancients regarded war dancing—solo war dancing—as very important to the development of a warrior.

In martial arts 'boxing' is practiced primarily by hitting mitts with a sympathetic partner. In contrast at boxing gyms the art is practiced by hitting air and bags while imagining an antagonist in front of you.

Currently, in America, most stick-fighting and blade-fighting is Asian-based, with the focus either on preset sequences utilizing an artificially compliant 'partner', or [less in-authentically] via 'feeder drills' in which partners practice sequential and sympathetic drills with the focus on the weapon. This process is one of artifice, of being mired in the object, the material, and is counter to the meditative process.

However, the stick-fighter who practiced solo hitting air and bags in an antagonistic mediation on fluidity in combat—he usually murders the stick-tappers when they meet in combat, because he has developed his combat serenity holistically, not separately from his skill set, sitting among wind chimes and wafting incense.

Some of us seek out places 'where life is scarce' as my otherwise unwise friend Bano used to say.

At the End of Masculine Time

When this deranged war-scarred killer and I met he told me that he respected me for being quiet, cool and 'for living in your own mind.'

When asked how I cultivated this habit I admitted that it was from walking at night, in extreme heat and cold, during storms, in back alleys, and in dangerous and deserted places; always seeking the least-traveled path to my destination. When called to explain myself I had to admit that this method of developing a serene demeanor was purely an accident, a byproduct of an alienated state. As a boy without friends I had sought lonely places as there I felt less alone. Then, upon moving to Baltimore city as it imploded in the early 1980s I found myself in a congested living space many miles from any remote area such as the woods I loved in Western Pennsylvania. I had not made a correlation until now, but it was at age 19, in the year of my grandfather's death, that I began walking the streets during nighttime thunderstorms, taking alleys, vacant lots and footpaths instead of sidewalks and streets.

Extreme weather is a gift of nature for the city dweller. I normally take the bus with 25 people at night. When the temperature dips below 10 it is me and two older men. My roommate was perplexed when I walked to work in 2 degrees the other night when he would have given me a ride. He does have a clue, as indicated by his comment, "I suppose pain and suffering is something you enjoy."

At the End of Masculine Time

It is usually not suffering. But a taste of the pain that once motivated our ancestors to drive beasts from caves, to capture fire, to wear animal hides, to invent the sewing needle, and otherwise assert themselves against nature is a healthy reminder of what we are, of what our masters no longer wish us to be.

This morning, as I went out for a stroll in zero degrees along the icy lanes of a city that has shut down, whose students do not go to school, whose TV news oracles declare the deadliness of the environment, mere miles from a county where it is against the law for a teenager to walk more than a mile to school, I have my best chance to get in touch with Grandpa Kern and his ancestors. Not only do I get to see the futility of Man's promise to himself to dominate nature in the form of broken water pipes and closed businesses and schools, but I get to enjoy the solitude of the primitive man who lived much of his life in silence except for the moans of the world. To my right, as I walked out into the middle of the dark street I could hear my American wind chimes, the painted sheet metal panels of a 100 year old barn being slowly torn apart by the undying world over which it once served as a symbol of domestication.

One walks by such a rotting edifice with hope, for since the patiently and soft-spoken wind is slowly but surely tearing down a long dead farmer's edifice of power, so might men—if they remain men—erode the equally rotten edifice of power once raised by shrill womanly men chanting their ideologies at the point of another man's gun.

The story of Western Man—right up until our fall into domestication—was one of defiance and conquest. Why, when we mediate, must we seek some Alien artifice, some phony Japanese or Tibetan dream space, when we can listen to the same music that our grandfathers and their grandfathers listened to all the way back into the dawn of our kind?

What is better than listening to the world moan?

In The Onion Field of the Soul

The Feminine Web of Rights and the Erosion of Masculine Virtue

At the End of Masculine Time

© 2015 James LaFond

"Here on the edge of time, at the end of all things."

-Craig Fraser, 2014

The most toxic notion that remains to emasculate what is left of Western Man is the notion of 'rights'.

Most of us think of rights in terms of 'what should be', or what would be 'just' and/or 'fair'.

For what it is worth, that statement of beliefs above is held by most Americans to accurately describe the concept of rights. But how useful is it as a practical application of the ideal in daily life?

'What should be' is, by definition, not reality, and is manifestly not 'what is.'

'Justice' is a perpetually argued concept that has religious origins but is currently nothing but a money pit for lawyers, with your 'sacred human right' nothing but the rope they tug parasitically upon. One needs to know what standards of justice prevail in the society he is enslaved to or dealing with. However, to trust in justice is supreme fallacy, and inevitably results in bitterness in the people I have known of that bent.

'Fairness' is currently the most favored way in which the postmodern American does express a notion of rights, being a vague sense that every person, no matter their character, crimes or contributions, deserve all of the same privileges. Fairness therefore reveals itself as the most toxic ideological pillar in human history. The key to understanding the notion of fairness is the associated notion of privilege.

A privilege is a good –an act, an object, an ongoing contract, etc.—enjoyed by a person simply because of who or what they are. A privilege therefore depends either on the tacit agreement of society [which is only possible in small scale communities], such as 'an elderly or sick person deserves to be taken care of,' or on threat of force.

A privilege becomes a right when the claim is backed by threat of force. This has historically been the province of the upper class who either monopolized warrior status, or have been in possession of fortunes sufficient to buy the services of the warrior, or currently his devolved cousin the police officer.

At the End of Masculine Time

Therefore, in any collective society greater than the size of an extended family, a right, is best defined as a privilege backed by threat of third-party force.

Therefore the concept of rights may be said to be the single most corrosive emasculating societal force, as it lends the illusion of power to one group of consumers—though in fact they have no agency and are ultimately dependent upon a third party for all things—in order that a class of producer may be enslaved. By overturning the exclusive rights of the tiny elite who used state power to prey upon the vast under class, the political revolutions of the Modern Age have ultimately resulted in a postmodern society in which every person is on one hand privileged and on the other hand a slave.

As the current understanding of rights originated with tribal traditions tacitly agreed upon to insure the welfare of those members who lacked the ability to physically assert their privilege through force [women, children, and the unwell] it is this man's opinion that it therefore follows that men living according to such a third-party threat system of privilege will, over time, adopt the behavior traditionally associated with women, children and the unwell.

At the End of Masculine Time

This concept is so misunderstood that even modern and postmodern thinkers who advocate 'might as right' entirely miss the point, that any system that relies for the enforcement of 'rights' via third-party threat, erodes the character and agency of the man benefitting from the privilege in question, and that eventually the system may—and therefore will—be steered against those members of society that it was once intended to favor.

A man's belief in his rights is a denial of his own masculine agency.

'What Smokes on God's Altar': Reconstructing the Theft of Western Man's Stolen Soul

"We say then that the Unmoved Mover is an eternal living being, the best of all, attributing to him continuous and eternal life."

-Aristotle, Physics, circa 340 B.C.

"Man has always worshipped one thing, himself, and himself only, either in the flesh or in the ghost—that is, in the non-flesh or the objective nothing—till he arrived at the transcendental Man, the superlative, the ideal of Himself."

-Richard F. Burton, Trieste, 1883

God's Shat Upon Altar

The first of the above definitions is an early deistic notion of God, with the line 'best of all' indicating Aristotle's concept being based on his culture's highest value, arête, or the virtues of a warrior, an ideal which harkens back to the earliest men.

The second definition is a modern Gnostic view of God as the sublime truth manipulated as masturbatory mind control; in other words the temporal [feminine] hijacking of the transcendental [masculine] notion of the Ideal for gross material gain rather than the expansion of Man's mind.

We, postmodern persons, generally misread the nature of ancient notions of God, largely because we misunderstand our own notion of God. Apart from the various allegorical god constructs such as Odin, Thor, Hera or Ishtar the actual functional notion of God—hinted at according to these allegorical traditions in their piecemeal way—is best described as the 'highest cultural ideal.' This Ideal will have an allegorical face [perhaps many], such as the Hebrew Yahweh, or the Olympian pantheon of the Hellenes. But it is incorrect to imagine, as we do, that what is venerated by the ancient theist—being the Ideal—is merely the same as the lingering artifice left to us.

Modernity brings unparalleled materialism stressing all levels of life, and most of all dragging down transcendent notions into the mire of artifice.

At the End of Masculine Time

A basic example is a god and his idol. The case against the idol is that a suitably degraded person will begin venerating the idol and lose contact with the god; lose touch with the Ideal even as he grasps the material representation.

This is alien to the modern way of thinking. Atheists, for instance, who reject the lingering idols of past allegorical traditions, and adopt a codified ethos of behavior and faith-based denial [a *belief* that there is no God] of the transcendent, are, in ancient terms, practicing a profound religiosity, that is not much different in ethics and function than the biblical Judaism of Moses. But, obsessed with artifice as he is, the atheist cannot see that his ideology is his Ideal and therefore his God.

An example from the combat arts world might better make the case. The prizefighter practices the art of combat, according to the ideal off effective expression. Once a certain noted combatant achieves hero status a virtual cult will grow up around his expression of the Ideal, and then inevitably, fall into artifice as his fighting life is reduced to mere mechanical curriculum, bereft of life, falling further from the Ideal with every generation of disciples, until finally there is a revolutionary figure who once again expresses the pure Ideal, and the process of heroization, deification, objectification, and eventual dead artifice begins anew.

Modernity and Emasculation

Those of us who have cared to observe have noted that psychological emasculation of the male human goes hand in hand with modernity. In Jack Donovan's No Man's Land, available through his website, the author does a diligent job of enumerating the academic assault on masculinity in the Post WWII period. I highly recommend that book to anyone who would like a better understanding of our current cultural view of men and masculinity.

Based on my research emasculation is as old as agrarian living, meaning the cultivation of the land as opposed to a hunting lifeway. We currently sit at the extreme end of this process, the denatured destination of Mankind, perched on the verge of a genderless society.

Contrast the primitive man with the modern man. The primitive man is made through self sacrifice at or after puberty. Just as nature changes the girl into a woman with the onset of menstruation, the boy changes himself into a man through an ordeal of self sacrifice, ether in collective trials such as wearing mitts full of stinging ants, or through lone vision quests and other austere rites of deprivation.

The epic poems of antiquity from Gilgamesh, to The Iliad, to the Odyssey, and finally Beowulf, make mention of early men being stronger than current men. Today, it can easily be seen that NFL players of the current era pale in terms of grit and toughness [the purity of their masculinity] to earlier players. So is this ancient poetic notion just a reflection of small cultural cycles, or does it hint at a long fall from a masculine Eden?

Might we take this notion of the masculine Ideal reduced to mere artifice—such as a loud voice, big muscles or a waxed mustache—and chart it from Early Modern to Postmodern times?

The Perennial Cult of Third Party Sacrifice

"The Devil went down to Georgia

looking for a soul to steal."

-Charlie Daniels

How did Western Man arrive at his current state, having made a Faustian bargain with The State to assume all of his masculine prerogatives, most notably his defense of himself and his family? It is in fact, the current actuality, that the human body is so worshipped, and that material ethics are so infused into our culture, that a man is not expected to protect himself or physically assert his agency in any way, unless this action is first explicitly sanctioned by The State [like being a police officer or soldier], and is even then subject to review. A Man's physical being is considered too important for him to entertain any risk. Indeed, as a man with no health insurance, I pay an extra tax to The State,

34

a penalty for the privilege of risk. A man's soul though—his ideal—is no longer of importance according to our current atheistic religious model.

In our Postmodern Atheistic Theocracy the entire world is God's Artifice, an idol bereft of its Ideal. By what specific process did America arrive at its soulless and genderless destination?

The key is our agrarian roots, which made our ancestors slaves to a fixed material order. The first order of business for colonists in North America was to wage war on the natural world, to kill the forest by ringing the trees, to hunt every animal great and small to extinction in drives intended to deprive the forest savages of their sustenance.

The agricultural ethic, or what Joseph Campbell called 'The Way of the Seeded Earth' was in direct opposition to 'the Way of the Animal Powers'. The final victory of the United States over the Native Americans circa 1990—facilitated by the near extinction of the plains bison—marked the end of a 10,000 year war between these two ideals.

The Way of the Animal Powers is masculine and vested in self sacrifice.

The Way of the Seeded Earth is maternal and vested in third party sacrifice. We see, from the Aztec practice of sacrificing enemy combatants, to Abraham being willing to butcher his son, to Yahweh consenting to the butchery of his divine son in the form of a human Christ, the maternal— and often race-based—ethic of third party sacrifice. Third party sacrifice takes the hero out of the realm of exemplary virtue wherein the hunter thrived, and casts him into the onion fields of oppression where the passive feminine mindset takes root and flourishes until every man becomes a woman at heart, as the ancient epic poems warned.

Permit me to track the process in America, but first we should define the devil's bargain struck between Man and State in regards to modernity and masculinity.

A Soul to Steal

What does modernity promise in return for emasculation? These things are enabled by material abundance. It is no surprise that material abundance gradually, and eventually totally, submerges the male spiritual Ideal beneath the female material Ideal. Materialism and the maternal Ideal—or Goddess—are inextricably linked.

The promise of modernity are:

1. You will not have to sacrifice as did your ancestors. Such expressive risk-based needs that arise will be suppressed through medication.

2. You will not be held to a code of behavior, as this is a state of ongoing sacrifice, and obviated by the third party sacrifice. Honor-based traditions such as dueling and the bonded word will therefore be abolished and replaced by counseling and contracts.

3. You will have more than your ancestors.

What society would agree to such an obviously unsustainable Devil's bargain that must collapse under the weight of its own expectations as soon as material abundance stops increasing?

This bargain makes intuitive sense to anyone raised in the Christian tradition, as it is entirely based on the notion of third party sacrifice, in which a life lived in utter undisciplined evil may be redeemed with a deathbed declaration of faith in the authenticity of Jesus' sacrifice. However, although

At the End of Masculine Time

Christianity has thus far served as the primary vector for the material Ideal, all 'seeded earth' faiths are suitable seedbeds for untrammeled materialism.

By the time this nation was founded circa 1780, its earliest colonists had been heroized, and served as the image of ancestral sacrifice.

A century later the Founding Fathers and their deistic iconography and Masonic cult imagery served as the self sacrificing heroized ancestral generation that justified the current state of ease, plenty, and increasingly risk averse lifeway.

A century later the dominant medium—Hollywood movies—portrayed the 'Winning of the West' by that generation of pioneers as the ancestral American sacrifice.

Now, at the End of Masculine Time, every form of media gushes at the 'Greatest Generation', heroizing even cooks and noncombatants from WWII, as the last generation of Americans who will ever be called upon to sacrifice. The declaration of 'The Greatest Generation' actually sets a time table for the dissolution of the United States, as being three generations removed from a descent into irreversible decline. For unless a declining people discover a new well of heroic figures to renew the cycle of the Ideal based upon the notion of third party sacrifice, cultural decline is assured. Ominously, with the cultural suicide of sterile feminists and denatured men wielding the final emasculatory blade, Western Culture is currently involved in the psychological butchery of its last generation of men, few as they may be.

One might reflect that it is a good thing for the quivering materialistic woman that Western Culture has evolved into through pursuit of the Ideal that some third party has made the last necessary sacrifice for our species, that there is not some other culture on the world stage; perhaps a culture with an ideal of individual warrior sacrifice. For if such a faith were extant on Planet Earth, based as it was on the belief that the warrior sacrifices now for the future of his people, how could our society—based as it is on our ancestors having already sacrificed for our current state of abundance—prevail in the long run?

The world is currently in the grips of a struggle that pits self sacrifice [the Jihadist with his AK-47] against the remaining material gains [U.S. drones and other forms of awesome military hardware and software] resulting from the sacrifice of the West's 'Greatest Generation.'

With the nature of the current ethos so infused with feminist ideals it seems that masculine notions will be more likely to survive in opposition to the social order than in support of it, which is hardly a recipe for continued Western hegemony. Fifty years ago this would seem like science-fiction. As this struggle winds up, and on, and finally down, perhaps men in the West might consider reclaiming their ancient 'Animal Powers' rather than continuing to hide behind their material God's oft shat upon altar.

Superman and the Plight of Orks: Commercial Heroics as a Force for Emasculation

Last week I went to the movies with my son to finish watching the J.R.R. Tolkien project from New Zealand, which consists of six long movies. Having read the Hobbit twice I much prefer the Rankin and Bass children's animation from the 1970s, as it was more in the spirit of the tale the old Brit told.

A female elf was inserted and the entire elvish presence in the story was grotesquely expanded, which makes sense, since elves are essentially denatured men. Of course black citizens of the Nordic lake town were also inserted. The focus on the dwarves was also feminized and denatured, by concocting a romance between the only dwarf that looks like he could have played guitar in a 1980s hair band and having him fall in cross-species love with the murderous elf babe, who was admittedly pleasing to the male eye.

As for the original story I always had a problem with the extreme domesticity of the adventurers and that fact that these lovable little chunkers never suffer PTSD after a year of nightmare battle. Honestly, Tolkien is emasculating enough. If I was rewriting the Hobbit I would write it as a patriotic call to ork kind, as the two ork generals were the only real believable warfighters in this entire battle heavy adaptation of the old children's tale. I rarely cheer in a movie, but I did cheer when that greedy little dwarf Thorin got gutted by the ork general Azog, who I think was played by a Polynesian dude.

The emasculation of war—and that is a huge topic—in this movie also amounts to its trivialization. A few flying faggots can wipe out armies of armored badasses without getting their hair messed up. Of course the good guys must always win. But the fact that they do so without sweating, bleeding, or needing another hairspray application in such video game inspired movies is truly obscene. Of course the elf chick basically wipes out an entire NFL team worth of armored monsters and threatens to murder her head of state, over her love affair with a person of a different species, not just race—species.

There was something about this that was nagging more than lack of realism. I am used to that, having avoided martial arts movies most of my life because of their lack of realistic combat. I did not figure out what was bothering me until a lady asked me who my favorite superhero was on Monday, and I had to face that pantheon of commercial propaganda deities.

Effective propaganda is not specific like the crude work of fascists and communists backed by naked power. Truly effective propaganda inculcates mores that assist the aspirations of our much more subtle brand of veiled hybrid power.

Ideally this propagandistic impulse is driven by consumerism—which will make it the best it can be—and will become so pervasive as to be self perpetuating.

The original broad message of Tolkien's work was this:

Ordinary people are capable of rising up and striking down a great evil so long as they are led

by a hereditary ruling class, and may then expect to return to a normal stress free life of cozy domesticity.

The Lord of the Rings was essentially a healing salve for the carnage of World War II [published 9 years after in 1954], and as such was an adaptation of Tolkien's earlier attempt to provide a comforting fantasy in the wake of the horrific World War I [the Hobbit, 1938]. The eagles are so obviously RAF Spitfires and the Nazgul so grotesquely Luftwaffe Studkas. It is no accident that both tales spend so much time reinserting the adventurers in their fairytale setting, as Tolkien was a WWI veteran himself.

What the makers of the Hobbit add to this is the notion that beautiful people [elves] can just pick up a piece of superior technology, get involved in a spur of the moment war against committed members of a warlike society, suffer nary a scratch, and walk away with only a care for their love life. Basically we have just piled 'and it's cool' on top of Tolkien's tea and biscuits message.

Superman is the American consciousness writ large. He is Aragorn and Frodo, righteous might and innocence. The key aspect is Clark Kent, unassertive ass-kissing functionary with no agency, submissive to women and the hierarchy—until, trouble comes. When trouble comes he morphs into Superman [anonymously, this is important] wipes out the bad guys, and returns to his ass-kissing life, taking no credit for saving the world.

In 1938 Superman was launched as a dark haired version of the Aryan Superman of Nazi myth, a capitalist alternative to that full time blonde warmonger; a part time combatant who is so superior that he could do what the Minute Men failed to do in New England against the British redcoats—win. Superman is the metaphor for the American male population that will toil industriously, submissive to his woman and the hierarchy he sits at the bottom of, and then go off to win victory, and return in anonymity and sink back into obscurity. The submissive anonymous nature of Clark Kent reveals Superman as propaganda targeting the working/warfighting underclass.

This is the genius of consumer culture based on advertising over substance; that your mind control engine is built right into daily living. Rather than go to church every Sunday to be psychologically harnessed to the social hierarchy as the patriot of

1776 did, the modern patriot is conditioned with his every waking breath.

Have a Coke, you deserve it.

Superheroes: God, Symptom, Villain?

An Anthology Inspired by Metal Head At Heart

At the End of Masculine Time

© 2015 James LaFond

The article **Superman and the Plight of Orks** has once again exposed this author as a hater of the self-love gods of American pop culture. I must say that I am additionally disgusted by the recent aggressive political correctness agenda demonstrated by major comic publishers—with gay, female and black versions of characters which seem to be a pure marketing ploy to expand the customer base. I mark superhero fiction as an indicator of social alienation.

From the beginning it has been a predominantly white male art form. The recent introduction of alternative heroes is certainly, on one hand, the driving of the stake into the heart of the reviled American Man of European descent, who has become the stock movie villain and TV dupe. On the other hand, it may mark a point at where these publishers have come to recognize that increasingly wider portions of society are just as alienated as the American Man was when the unconquered land that had defined him was replaced by a time clock and an office chair. If this later notion is true we should see a rise in black and female superhero villains in proportion to the new hero offerings.

At the End of Masculine Time

At its root I see the superhero phenomena as a resurrection of the polytheistic impulse in civilized humanity [Which is totally misunderstood by moderns and post-moderns and needs its own article]. When Man went from hunter, to nomad, to settled civilian he lost his animistic connection to the nameless world of spirits. Ancestor worship was retained in the form of gods—often deified ancestors with mythological links to natural phenomena and the cosmos—and the gods of the conquering tribes outranked the gods of the defeated tribes. This dynamic pushed the mythic cultural heritage down the cosmological pyramid until each locality had its own venerated being—or in some cases their god had been literally demonized. In ancient Hellas three boxers became minor gods, replete with virgin birth legends.

Aristotle saw these 'civic' gods as no better than children's tales, yet, recognized their usefulness in encouraging civic cohesion, even as he searched for The Cause Uncaused or the Unmoved Mover, as he conceptualized ultimate divinity. As the ages of empire began with his star pupil's [Alexander] world conquest, local gods died out and the process of syncretism folded god into god, into god into GOD.

At the End of Masculine Time

Atheism, stoicism, cynicism and other philosophies also filled this psycho-social breach in the minds of the educated elite. But among the common people there was still a need that came to be realized ingeniously by the Catholic Church in the cult of Saints, which was essentially a selling point for barbarian pagans who still cleaved to old gods, but found resonance among the perennial downtrodden in established regions. Eventually the cult of saints would even recognize American Indian deities.

What I see in the growth of the superhero phenomena and its accelerated growth in modern and postmodern society—primarily among young males but now among all genders and age groups—is the old patron deity impulse rising from the crumbling dust of this decaying culture. Notably evangelical Christians and an Islamic publisher have come to understand and even co-opt superhero imagery. In American Sniper, one of Chris Kyles' SEAL team members loves reading Punisher comics. The team even paints Punisher imagery on their uniforms and vehicle.

As meaning washes away from life and the spiritual erosion of domesticity gains momentum do it yourself gods; being anthropomorphic reflections of the portions of our humanity that we sense are being taken away—most importantly masculinity—will continue to rise into the common consciousness.

Or so this nut-job author claims.

Below are the links to articles I have posted on this site that touch on the superhero question, from oldest to most recent. The first and third are really about the mythic basis of the art form. I recall writing an article critical of Batman and Superman in which I was taken to task over lumping Batman in with the flying cosmic steel beam by a reader, but could not find it.

Metal Head At Heart Library

Into The Mind's Eye Of Mythic Hellas

Four Minutes To Midnight

'The Secret Cause Of All Suffering'

'No Superhero Story'

__Conan As A Superhero?__

__The Dark Right__

__Thor Gets A Sex Change!?!__

__In The Age Of Black Superman__

__'Dat Gay ATV'__

__Superman And The Plight Of Orks__

'What Use Is It?'

'What Good Is It To Be the Better Man When The Machine Wins in the End': A Man Question from George

At the End of Masculine Time

"You have written so much—and convincingly—about better warriors: Vikings, Indians, Confederates, Germans in World War One and Two, being better men then their opponents. But in the end they get eaten up by numbers and industrial capacity. So what is the use; why be a better warrior, why even reclaim your masculinity, when in the end The Machine wins and you are left with nothing?"

Thanks for the thoughtful question George. This is probably the only question that I have fielded on this site that I could have answered at 12 years old, and which does not reflect an opinion that has ever changed in this matter. This surety has resulted in my being lax and not addressing this crux of a manly matter in either of my last three non-fiction books. It is times like this when a writer misses having an editor to slap him across the face and say, "But what about the obvious? Hello, anybody home!"

The Machine wins the material struggle, not the transcendent one. Agamemnon won the Trojan War, not Hector or Achilles. Three thousand years later we read the Iliad and half of us can't remember the name of the fat rich bastard that fought that war for material gain. Who do we remember, who do we revere?

Achilles owns the book and Hector—both victims of Agamemnon's cupidity and greed—gets the last line. Every Roman soldier wanted to be Hector. Even Alexander the Great wanted to be Achilles, gave away kingdoms to his men out of fear that he might become Agamemnon. Even Agamemnon would have rather been Achilles!

Achilles means 'Sorrow-of-the-people'. So, just as he, doomed in his defiance and rage, remained the beating heart of martial culture throughout antiquity, our own modern defeated warriors live still, even in the hearts of their enemies' descendents.

The Apache people spent 400 years kicking the shit out of better armed white men. Finally, when General Myles hired enough Apaches to track Geronimo and his refugee women and children down, and end the thing at last, at 5,000 to 60 odds, one might speak of the old Apache as having lost, having won nothing. He got sent to a swamp from his high dry mountains to rot away and be carted around as a trophy.

At the End of Masculine Time

But, fifty years later, when the grandsons of his conquerors had to jump into Occupied Europe to fight the hard cases that had already slaughtered millions of brave Russians, what did they scream? They screamed Geronimo—and he had been their forefathers' enemy. Even so, he had become what the American fighting man measured himself against.

The Machine does not win the battle, it *is* the battle; the stage the warrior strives on. The Machine cannot win, nor can its functionaries, and wards, and suckling children, anymore than the corrupt sport of boxing, or its fat cat promoters, or its snarky announcers, or its beer drinking fans, can win a boxing match. Only a boxer can win, and yes, the stage eventually expels or devours him, and that is the whole point, because he cannot live forever until he dies.

'Look At Me!': The Plight of Weak Women in Harm City

Yesterday afternoon at 4:40 p.m. I was walking home from the diner, five doors from the house where I rent a room. This secondary street gets a lot of foot traffic to the bus stop on the main drag. On the other side of the street headed my way was a young lady I see often. She is five six, about 150, caramel colored and hour glass shaped. She is younger than my youngest son so I make certain to look straight ahead and do not look over at her. She is uncomfortable around men. The first time I passed her on the street she was terrified.

This young lady dresses modestly even in summer, when most black girls dress like they should be pole dancing. She crosses her arms in front of her breasts when she walks, hunching her shoulders slightly. She cannot, however hide her hips, and they were her undoing on this graying winter day.

At the End of Masculine Time

As I turned to walk up to the house I heard a car stop quickly. It was a small economy car driven by a braided hair man in his mid 20s. He had screeched to a halt a block past her. He was now looking back over the seat at her hips getting farther away, which apparently would not do.

I stopped and watched instead of entering the house.

He sped in reverse until he was even with her.

She hunched her shoulders and slowed but kept walking.

He—or perhaps a passenger—said something through the passenger window and she shook her head 'no' and walked on unsteadily.

He got out of the car and slammed the door, which caused her to shudder and stop.

He was about 5', 10" and 140 pounds, and I was pretty certain I could stop him. I could not, however, see through the tinted windshield to determine if he had an accomplice, and he was now too far back down the street for me to see through the driver's side. That had me bothered so I picked up the gold-painted cast iron antique clothes iron that we use to prop the screen door open when carrying groceries, beer, or drunken wenches over the threshold.

The girl was frozen stiff, looking straight ahead, seemingly talking to herself or counting.

He then yelled, "Bitch, look at me!"

She looked trembling over her shoulder and he threw his hands out to the side and shouted, "You could a had this girl!"

She held her arms crossed more tightly and squinted as she batted her eye lashes over her shoulder, fighting back tears and choking on some kind of apology.

He then scoffed at her callously as he waved the back of his hand at her in disgust. "Get on down the road you stuck up fuckin' bitch!"

The thug then slid into his car, slammed the door shut, and screeched wheels as he sped through the stop sign at about 40.

The young lady was on her way, hunched forward and wrapping her arms across her chest like she was freezing.

At the End of Masculine Time

I am often critical of the loud, abrasive and violent nature of black women in Baltimore. I would say a quarter of black females I run into are hyper-violent. Most of the remainder are coldly haughty, comporting themselves with a too-good-for-you homeboy scowl, that is so ubiquitous I often expect to run into a display of ebony frowns at the dollar store. It is rare to run into a black girl with the passive mannerisms and timidity of a cultured white woman. After seeing harassment of our dainty neighbor I am reminded why nice girls don't last long in this sewer of sour souls.

If I had a vagina in this town I wouldn't go anywhere without a steel hairpin in my wig and a rusty razor taped to the back of my smart phone.

I won't normally help a black defend against other blacks —even when it's a gang of older boys beating a younger one. But I could not have watched this animal put his hands on this girl. I am designed with an urge to defend women against such aggression even as I show callous disregard for weak men in such dire straights. In today's PC climate that was a damning admission. So I must amend my 'Let the Weak Fall' credo, to, "Let the Weak Fall, unless she's cute and keeps her mouth shut."

I'm glad he settled for insults and went on his unsavory way.

Where is that speeding dump truck with failing brakes when you need it?

'Let the Weak Fall': Or Let Her Get My Beer and Rub My Shoulders: A Column on Rejecting Asian-based Combat Arts

"Give me a mongoloid nut that has been beating something with a stick in his basement for six moths over a graduate of one of these escrima programs any day. I'm betting on that guy! Even the stick-gods [Rico and Aaron] that murdered us, they did it with power, and by dominating the combat space with movement. My experience is that combat is a lot more about conditioning; this [makes beating heart motion], than how many moves you can do in class. David and Gabriel both know their arts are not directly applicable in combat—that's why they pointed us in your direction. What we do in Modern Agonistics is throw what doesn't work out the window and apply what's left. You need to get back to that principal."

-Charles M. 1/27/15, after coaching his coach

Unburdening Your Masculine Nature from Sissy Artifice

As our readers are well aware, I'm quite literally a knucklehead; a fighter and coach. My thought process in all things is infected with the ethos of the combatant. This was the means by which I—as a childhood wimp—reinvented myself as a little savage, a 'Don't tread on me' cartoon anti-hero in sneakers.

By age 15 it become obvious to me that I did not have the athletic capacity to be a welterweight contender, something that my coach was very upfront about. I did, however, posess a measure of menace; had established myself as a maniac not to be messed with. Ever since then I have striven to maintain this identity through training and competing in combat sports. I have also devoted myself—since moving to the predation zone known as Baltimore Maryland—to developing a dualistic set of social and anti-social skills to obviate the need to 'fight' in this urban setting.

Toward these ends I have alternately trained in, coached, organized, written, and mentored in the area of the combat arts, which encompasses combat sports [which I am involved in], practical survival training [which I am involved in] and martial artistry [which I am not involved in, though remain associated with due to the need to share training and venue facilities with martial arts programs.]

I have served as a coach for numerous martial arts programs, programs that teach, promote and practice arts that I do not engage in, but have a functional understanding of, as I have competed against, cross-trained with, and re-trained many practitioners of Asian-based martial arts. I have formed real brotherhoods with leaders in the martial arts community—fringe characters though they may be in their own fraternity.

Over the past five years I have devoted much of my effort to developing a format by which fighters might be able to compete against martial artists in stick-fighting and knife-dueling. These weapons are practical items of everyday self-defense and their competitive use is not governed by any political commission. Since all Asian-based martial arts deal with the simple arm-length stick and knife as a weapon of interest to the self-defense practitioner I believe that contact weaponry is the natural meeting place and middle ground for the combat athlete and the martial artist. Toward that end I have done much over the past two years to compromise my training ethics to embrace the more serious programs in the martial arts community.

This effort is now at an end, as this past week, an experiment that has run for six months in my concussed mind has finally concluded.

The Anglo-Asian Combat Experiment

Back on July 5th Erique [sober] Charles [buzzed] and I [trashed] fought in a 'drunken agon'. I unexpectedly came out on top. Since that time the three of us have gotten together on a monthly basis for light sparring work. Charles was busy working seven days a week so has not, until this past month, been available for regular training. In the meantime, Erique and I did our training under a martial arts guru who teaches the Filipino art that is the closest thing to the freestyle American stick-fighting and blade combat we engage in. Unlike most members of his fraternity he believes in our free-style format and would like some of his students to engage with us. He has even judged events we have fought in. He is not clannish or insular, but seeks to expand his knowledge.

So, for six months Erique and I have engaged in martial arts, with his younger mind and body proving more able to absorb the instruction. His wife has also gotten involved in the training. Indeed, since I was invited to this school as an assistant coach two years ago, and sparred with the entire class—taking it easy on them, not hurting them, and doing everything I could to assuage the damaged egos of the young studly hunks of athletic flesh that proved unable to touch me in sparring— young men have avoided this class like it were a leper colony. What little interest is being shown is coming from women and older men.

One fascinating item of discovery has been that I—a fighter with over 600 bouts with a roughly 50/50 record against pro-level practitioners of these arts—have proven incapable of learning the ever more elaborate non-contact sympathetic sequences that comprise the learning format. Erique chuckles every time I fail midpoint in one of these drills, and recently said, "You know every time you screw up in this drill it's because your instinct to hit me is trying to get through."

Erique, an amateur level fighter with a couple dozen bouts under his belt, is steadily learning the non-contact system of weapons choreography which we are told is the key to success in the full-contact insanity of no-holds-barred combat.

The most interesting development is that his dainty little wife is now instructing me. For she, as has been my experience with coaching women, finds it much easier to learn sympathetic patterns in a non-contact context than do most men. In fact, the art of Kenpo, which has the most extensive and complex training sequences in all the martial arts, is extremely popular among male musicians—

including the late Elvis Presley. At this point, as she coached me on a Filipino boxing method that requires the defender to throw three to five hand checks against a single punch [an output disparity which the best boxers in history have not been able to achieve against the most mediocre opponents] with full knowledge that I can line up all of the MMA studs in this school and KO them in stick fights, and that my boxer Craig could level every amateur kick boxer in this school, I came to the Asian-Anglo impasse that I have so often tread upon for those four decades.

First let me be clear that this is the best school of its kind in the area, and one of the best in the region. This woman, who could not prevent me from throwing her over my shoulder and carrying her out the front door, is—according to the Filipino 'martial arts' interpretation of combat ability—my superior. According to the Asian-based martial arts perspective—or at least according to the manner in which these arts have been marketed to the sissy American public—I should not be able to defend myself against her, her husband, the young karate guy that stopped in to try it out, or our master. In reality, only Erique has the guts to mix it up with me in combat.

Crawling Out of the Rabbit Hole

So, taking away this perspective of myself as theoretically unable to sustain myself in combat due to the hundreds of combats I have been in, and all of the doctrines these experiences have taught me to eschew, I show up at our freestyle Modern Agonistics venue the next day. Keep in mind that I have pursued this cross training for two reasons:

1. To attract some of the many fit young men that my friend the martial arts guru has under his banner to compete against fighters I train, for the purpose of mutual growth

2. To support the man's program that I basically trashed. For the week after I easily schooled all of his young athletes on the mat, he made his son—a godlike physical specimen who is a successful MMA fighter and is certified to teach fighting with the very same weapon I fight with in my uncertified manner—spar with me. Now, in Western martial arts you do not spar guys at the same level, lest it turn into a fight. But in Asian-based arts sparring is not seen as a development tool but as competition. His boy brought it, brought it so well that I was not

able to simultaneously protect myself and him. I was forced to beat him like a red-headed step child. In Western combat this is a compliment; that I had to handle you roughly. I duly complimented him but his ego was maimed and he stopped showing interest in the weapons aspect of the program. Without discussing this point of mutual embarrassment the guru offered to teach me his system so I could instruct as an assistant. Unfortunately my ADHD and dyslexia makes this impossible.

My purpose for engaging in this 'art' is now at an end. However, I still wanted to do what I could to support this very kind, tolerant and knowledgeable instructor in the growth of his program.

One thing that was echoing in my mind was my friend David Lumsden's critique of the martial arts genius who had developed the type of system that this teacher uses, and is certified to teach the very same systems. His name is Dan Inosanto, the assistant of Bruce Lee. David told me that, "Dan was the curriculum guy. He was a school teacher."

It now makes so much sense to me that women pick up on these sympathetic non-contact drills so easily, when—even after Erique and I learn them—

our more naturally gifted fighters, Brett, Craig, and Charles, are totally unable to absorb combat lessons in this theoretical form.

The Test of Art

The test was on as I entered our Host's school and saw one of the guru's young men there. If, after two years, we could finally manage to attract one of his 'artists' to our fighting venue perhaps it was not for naught, and it would make sense for me to continue networking at that school.

As I cleaned the mats the visiting martial artist refused all of Charles' offers to spar on the mat. Charles even brought out a suit of armor for the guy to wear and promised not to hit him. Still the martial artist shrank in fear. He did eventually come out on the mat and 'teach' Erique some joint locks. This was rude, and is the very womanly refuge of the martial artist afraid of contact—the offer to teach tricks. I wanted to go over to him and offer him the contents of my wallet if he could slap one of these locks on me, even rehearsed my line. But this would have gotten ugly and was not my place. I'm on the staff at this school and am honor bound not to lay down challenges, only accept them.

The test now came. With Charles having walked the elliptical at the fitness center looking at the sweaty sculpted behinds in front of him—hardly ever picking up a stick in the past six months—how would he do against Erique and I? We had been practicing 'martial arts' for six months, practicing with these very sticks that he had rarely picked up since I beat his ass with one on the 5th of July? if the art was valid Erique would do best, followed by me, and at the expense of Charles.

Charles took it easy on Erique for an hour before the much stronger and recently artistically schooled man literally melted into the mat.

The visiting martial artist shrank in fear, scurried to a safe corner.

I stepped up with Charles and he toyed—like Jerry the mouse would if he were as big as Tom the cat—with me for an hour and a half until I felt like Fred Sanford having a coronary. The most irritating thing was that I was using—without thinking about it—stroke combinations that were suicidal, that had worked their way into my muscle memory from the martial art I was practicing. I was partly into the process of deprogramming my fighting mind, of becoming an Anglo-Asian American choreographic culture vector.

Every time a stick stroke comes up in FMA practice that is manifestly not an effective 'stick' strike, and I question the master teaching this he will always say, "Well, the stick represents a sword."

"Why then do we not practice with a stick that is shaped like a sword?"

"Because the Filipino's were not allowed to have weapons under Spanish occupation so practiced with sticks."

Sorry, I thought we sank the Spanish fleet off Manila 118 years ago. So there we are, compromising practical combat ability in order to preserve some distant people's culture of oppression.

It then came to me on the matt, that I had cheated my masculine nature, had been allowing the feminized Asian-based art to creep into my combat matrix. The syncopated mnemonic teaching exercises developed by a Filipino-American California educator to teach Sissy America the art of his ancestor's nation—though a booming commercial success—ripped the balls out of stick-fighting. In fact Filipino men are notably absent from the toughest FMA and freestyle stick-fighting venues, despite it being their national sport. Real Filipinos would rather watch American-style boxing, and do!

I thought back to the white men of the 70s taking up Japanese karate instead of boxing because they feared competing with a black man.

I thought back to the scores of Americans who have come to me for reprogramming after earning awards in an Asian-based art, and decided that my diplomatic experiment had run its course, and the damage I have done to my combative mind must be reversed.

The Religion of Fighting Like a Nun

The subject of this column, 'Let the Weak Fall' is about the rejection of the feminizing influence of Asian-based martial arts in postmodern America. It is firmly my belief that the commercialization of art forms designed to promote smaller and weaker people as superior physical combatants, have run their destructive course to an irredeemable degree. Wing Chun [Beautiful Springtime] for instance, is said to have been developed by a Chinese nun as a means to beat up men, and is regarded as the most effective traditional Asian martial art by a wide margin, yet has proven ineffective in cage combat. It was, however, the basis for Bruce Lee's art so dominates large tracts of masculine American culture.

The link below shows the merits of Wing Chun set against the merits of being Russian. Many other videos show Wing Chun practitioners more recently winning cage fights and other open venues. You will usually see in these that the Wing Chun practitioner who wins is either a better athlete, bigger, or departs from his art and fights in a hybrid manner. One of my best friends teaches Wing Chun religiously. But I think that the way the art is generally promoted according to the notion that physicality and conditioning is second to art and technique is a dangerous myth, as Igor below demonstrates.

http://www.bing.com/videos/search?q=wing+chun+vs+mma&FORM=VIRE3#view=detail&mid=AD70646FD1BAEAE87E8CAD70646FD1BAEAE87E8C

At the End of Masculine Time

There is also a good Australian YouTube fight of a kickboxer beating the piss out of a Wing Chun man. Again, that fight did not come down to 'style' as all Asian-based instructors will claim, but, like the fight above, came down to the bigger more athletic man imposing his will, on the smaller less phyiscal adherent to the ancient nun's art.

I am a mediocre boxer and managed to frustrate one of the best area Wing Chun fighters in sparring to the point where he reverted to Tae Kwon Do and kicked me in the head, then reverted further to Chicago-style boxing he learned as a kid and tore apart my jaw. This is the Wing Chun pattern of a physically superior or better all around fighter lending his credit to the nun's art in return for her gift of serenity. I find nothing wrong with this, and am only pointing out that it must be understood for what it is.

When Craig and I attended a Wing Chun seminar we were pitied by the Wing Chun practitioners for our inability to fight—were totally unable to grasp the drills. Then it came time to spar. I sent Craig out there with instructions to take it easy and not hurt anyone and it looked like a slaughter house for teddy bears with Craig wielding the meatsaw. No amount of female prevaricating will elevate the man above the realities of combat.

Most such programs are now actually women's confidence building and children's day care programs with scant room for men. Shockingly the most manly oriented programs that are not MMA focused are Wing Chun classes. A look at the physical and mental make up of the top Wing Chun guys compared to other traditional teachers shows a stronger more thickly built and more aggressive man. These guys—like my friend—often switch to Wing Chun to calm their demons down, to stop getting in senseless street and bar fights. They actually use this art as a way to get away from fighting and its many negative social connotations. Then their success is interpreted as the success of a nun's art. This is the American way of looking at the material artifice rather than the transcendent element—the fighting spirit of the man. The fact that the most macho and usually most feared traditional Asian-based martial arts practice a nun's style of boxing should say something about the overall martial arts setting.

Let the Weak Fall

I have, in the past, agreed to coach women and children, as a favor, as a means of practicing the pure art, as a way to keep busy coaching as the mangina hordes slumber in their video game dens. It was a way for me to practice coaching while waiting for the American Man to reawaken and place his video controller in the bin designated for sanitary napkins.

No more.

Henceforth I only deal with men. This weak I will begin a program called 'Combat for Men' at my Host's school. There will not be many takers, as being a Man is Taboo in our society. But it's a start.

Despite the combat experience, and combat orientation of our instructor, the arts that he has been taught and stands honor-bound to perpetuate are structured in such a way as to encourage sympathetic choreography, and thus encourage female and mangina participation at the expense of realizing the combative needs of men.

I thank him. I honor him. But I walk on and *Let the Weak Fall.*

For more on this perspective, and to get a better idea as to what this column is going to be about, read ***Why I Am Not A Martial Artist***.

If you like this article you might wish to checkout my book **Letters from Planet Meathead** available at this link.

http://www.amazon.co.uk/Letters-Planet-Meathead-Fighters-Postmodern/dp/1503353591

Comments

fatmanjudo   January 30, 2015 8:33 PM EST

I can't speak for any other club than the one I attended but we approached it as a learning art and not really a competitive art. It is divided into ground and standing. Competence in one does not entail competence in the other. The learning curve is much less steep for ground "rolling" versus stand up throws. Most people arrive with some experience in wrestling and are thus familiar with the body contact. They have to be taught what not to do and be told to tap early and often. Two can roll all out with little worry about serious injury. If one "wins" you are expected to show your opponent what you did. If there is a large weight or strength disparity then the superior is told to rely on technique and not muscle. Easier said than done but this is encouraged. Most people really like to roll and there is an infinite amount of new things to learn. Any pain is generally gone after a couple beers.

New People do not like the throws though. There is no prior experience to build off of. They must be learnt from step one. First you must be taught brakefalls. It takes a long time to get the basic throwing form correct. You spend a lot of time hitting (or missing) the crash pad. We call the stand up sparring roundori. It is always supervised by a blackbelt. You are told to go 50% which lasts for a few minutes and the next thing you know your going 110%. The third man keeps it controlled. Newbys either don't do roundori or are pared with people who are competent and can dial it down. Basically they have a steep hill to climb and roundori is not useful until a basic competence is acquired.

It is also painful to be thrown if you are not competent in brakefalls.

Thus their time is better spent throwing an uki or grip fighting where they fight for superior position which is needed prior to executing a throw.

Pax

Fatmanjudo   January 29, 2015 7:47 PM EST

My instructor has similar gripes concerning pre

versus post 1967 judo. Don't even get him going on about current judo rules. However the nice thing about the grappeling arts is that guys that like grappeling grapple. That is to say if you show up with a move that works while rolling they are going to learn it despite the moves provinence. Of course this does not mean you can use it in competition, but we will learn it. Its the rolling that makes the grappling arts so effective. You cant fake it.

Your observation concerning psychological hurdle of getting punched is right on. There is a similar hurdle to being thrown. I have worked out at a boxing club and its the getting punched in the head which is difficult for me to do. Unfortunately. One cannot progress without the pain. I just try to keep it to a minimum and work with guys who have nothing to prove and are unquestionably better than me. It's their ability and lack of ego which allows them control. A control I do not have because only people with skill can "dial it down". As I have no boxing skill there is nothing to dial down. Instead only on and off.

Your complaint about watering down skills for women and children is nothing more than a critique of capitalism. Capitalism is all about "having the form of godliness, but denying the power thereof." Sorry about the long note. Your post just got my brain thinking. Which is often both dangerous and nonproductive. Pax

Finding Your Combat Space: How To Select A Worthy Training Venue

Below is a culling progression, beginning with generalities and ending with specifics.

1. Looking for a low rent facility will steer you towards schools or gyms that are less commercial. Generally basement, loft and recreation center operations will be more focused on combat than profit.

2. If you wish to consider a program located in a high rent facility go for a free standing building. Avoid mall and strip mall locations, unless you have a referral for a coach or instructor at this location, and or the owner has invested in visible equipment; such as a ring, cage, bag array, mats.

3. Never ever enter a school that has after school vans.

4. Avoid programs that cater to women, children and families. You are looking for a wolf pit, not a petting zoo.

5. There must be appropriate protective equipment: grappling schools must have mats, boxing gyms gloves and headgear; weaponry programs protective masks and gloves. The coach should be able to answer a battery of questions off the top of his head concerning the equipment use and properties, particularly if the equipment is not worn.

6. Facilities where striking arts and weapon arts are practiced must have striking apparatus: bags, posts, ropes, dummies, mitts, etc.

7. Weaponry programs that are non-contact are to be avoided.

8. Weaponry training that focuses on tapping weapons together should be avoided. You would not pay a boxing coach that primarily taught fighters to punch the opponent's gloves, or a grappling coach that focused on actually attacking and damaging the opponent's uniform, would you?

9. Boxing gyms and contact weaponry clubs should pair new fighters up for sparring against the best fighters in the gym. Paring off new fighters to spar with each other is either reckless of the new fighters' safety or done to build false confidence.

10. Any type of combat art should only teach basic fundamentals to beginners. The longer a boxing coach waits to teach the hook, the better he is. The boxing trainer who teaches the hook in the first lesson is incompetent as a coach, no matter how good his hook might be. A stick or knife fighting instructor who teaches disarms on the first lesson, or before the student has acquired proficient mobility and weapon usage, is selling fantasy. Likewise, be suspicious of a grappling coach who teaches joint locks, chokes and submissions before position, control and transition. Lack of

fundamentals instruction is the mark of either incompetence or fraud.

Few training venues are perfect. However, any venue that does not have any of the big potential negatives above attached to it should be well worth your while.

A Boxing B.S. Detector

A Quick Test Of Your Perspective Boxing Coach's Knowledge And Commitment

This is boxing, so we are not just talking about knowledge, but commitment too. You might be dealing with a coach who simply declines to coach you properly due to the fact that he does not care about you or your progress. If you are going to a martial arts instructor for your boxing and he fails one of the tests below it is probably lack of knowledge. The common mistake Asian-based martial arts instructors make is to get boxing instruction—usually on the Jeet Kune Do circuit—in seminar format, or at an MMA club, or white collar boxing program, as opposed to a real boxing gym. The fact that boxing is not about knowledge or a complete skill set, but is about psychology and an applied yet forever incomplete skill set, is lost on martial artists in general.

If you are going to a boxer or boxing coach for your hand skills and he fails at some point on this test he might be a subpar coach. Or, he might not care about you.

Once you have been coached in boxing you may rate your coach on this descending scale, from 10 to 2 and below. This is all about your first session, and what you are coached on. This is a good assessment of your coach's overall knowledge of boxing and/or his commitment to you developing functional boxing ability.

Below is the score to the left and what it means to the right. Less is better, more is worse. This only concerns the information you were given and the work you were made to perform in your first session.

-Specific defenses against a punch are properly shown after you have been instructed on the punch. If you are shown an active defense to a punch you have not yet been instructed on, deduct 1 from the score.

-Subtract 1 from the score for every jab variation shown in the first session [there are 7 variations].

-Cut the score in half for each of the three elements in the 10 score that are absent.

Boxing B.S. Barometer

10: guard [posture or stance, your structural defense], movement [your passive defense], the jab [your bridge between offense and defense]

8: also the right hand [usually shown because he is afraid you will get bored, I have done this to retain interest among white collar boxers]

6: also the hook

4: also the upper cut

2: also an additional punch variation of the right, the hook, or the uppercut

So, if your coach shows you how to stand, how to move, and how to properly throw one basic jab, than that is a 10. Anything else he shows you lowers the base score or causes a deduction in his base score.

On the other hand, if you go to a Jeet Kune Do school or MMA club, and they show you the guard, and then how to throw the four basic punches without going over movement, and go over the defense to each punch—which is precisely how boxing is normally taught in a martial arts setting—then they score a base of 4, cut in half for neglecting movement, for a total of 2. If they add a variation of the jab that drops their score to 1.

Note: this barometer only applies if you are not an experienced boxer. If you have already trained or fought he will want to see what you can do and encourage you to demonstrate your skills before determining what he can add without messing up your positive aspects, and what needs to be corrected. The above table is intended for the novice or martial artist to assess a coach.

I will cover more boxing martial arts chicanery in The Boxer as Uke, coming soon to a computer terminal in front of you, right where the obedient martial artist believes his antagonist will always be.

This article came out to 666 words so I have written his sentence for no rational reason.

'What About Your Fight Record?'

A Man Question From Charles

"How do you know how many fights you've had? It seems like a stretch. Did you count sparring? Why don't I have a record?"

With all of the charlatans in the 'stick-fighting' world out there it is a fair question to ask. Let's set aside my disastrous boxing record for now. The record you were discussing after our last training session currently stands as so:

At the End of Masculine Time

From 1998 thru 2014 James has fought 668 stick bouts for a record of 448 wins, 168 losses and 52 draws.

From 2002 thru 2013 James fought 221 blunt machete duels for 116 wins, 86 losses and 19 draws.

The stick record is fights against everybody, some not very good fighters included. The machete duels were only against top fighters. I am actually a better blade man than stick man, so this shows what a difference quality of opposition makes in a record.

I know how many fights I've had and what the outcomes where because I either kept track during a private meet—like when Aaron and I met for 4 1 hour beatings of this guy, which netted me 1 win out of 29 fights. In the case of a pubic meet—or at our July 5th slobber knocker where I was drunk, I had my girl keep track of the stick fights on a note pad, which I found in my pocket the next day. In other cases I have viewed films of bouts from events, like in our May 2013 agon.

Mathematically I am somewhere just above an earth worm. But, this is just adding. Earth worms can add. Hell, dirt can add! From 1998 through

At the End of Masculine Time

2004 I kept track of everyone's fights. When we started having open meets I was overwhelmed and decided to keep my own record going, as it served a much bigger purpose than my own bragging rights.

Records are good and bad. An example of what is bad about records is managing a fighter so that he has a perfect one, and thereby not testing him, like in boxing. Another example of how record keeping is bad comes from my years of training as a boy with weights. I became obsessed with how much I could lift, and tried to break certain barriers.

At age 15 and 143 pounds I had the following stats:

-dips, 127 [75 with 50 pounds tied to my waist]

-rope climb without using legs, 16 feet in 4 seconds, could do it at progressively slower times four times in a row without a standing rest at the bottom

-pull ups, 18

-chin ups, 21

-pull ups behind the back, 14

-Olympic barbell snatch, 145 pounds

-Olympic barbell clean and jerk, 155 pounds

-barbell curl, 120 pounds

-bench press 195 pounds

I destroyed my right shoulder trying to turn the 200 pound corner in the bench press. Now I can't do a single dip and a pull up is agony. Getting out of bed is like getting off the floor after you knocked me down last Sunday. The point is this ego-centric record caused me to ruin a really good set of shoulders.

In late 1998 Chuck Goetz and I wanted to start fighting with sticks. We had fought with knives in kill bouts and using different point systems for a year. Until I found the Lumsden brothers in 2002 and Aaron in 2005 no one in Baltimore would spar with or fight us—nobody had done it that we knew of. Before we began recruiting people we decided to do a study of 140 bouts.

We called a stick-fight over when one of us had taken 5 hard clean shots. The reasoning was that no one I knew of from my violence study had taken 5 blunt weapon strokes without being incapacitated. In some cases the person survived dozens of strokes before going out. But in no case did someone who was hit five times with a blunt weapon not become incapacitated at some point before or after the fifth stroke.

Chuck and I wanted information, numbers. We did the first 140 fights with rattan, white oak, ash wood, wax wood, and once with 1 and ¼ inch foot long steel pipes. We fought in the park in front of homeless guys and Mexican landscapers who gave us feedback. They noted that the fights with the more dangerous materials lasted longer and had little action. We settled on rattan and have stuck with it ever since.

My record includes bouts fought according to the following methods: 5 point, weapon only submission, NHB submission, MMA, FMA, freestyle, gladiatorial, double-stick, stick and dagger [FMA and freestyle].

The longest and most grueling stick fight was a 10 minute submission bout with Chuck.

The nastiest one was a roughly two minute 5 point bout against Aaron in which he broke his stick on me, bent the main bar of my helmet and disarmed me.

At the End of Masculine Time

The quickest stick fight was against you young man, when I took your forehand in the left lat, and snaked your stick away as I smacked you in the temple in front of a dozen young college ladies.

This begs the sparring question. You had been murdering me in sparring but choked in front of that gathered vagina. The next week, when Cory and I arrived at the school and you were already there, I noticed he had not brought gear. When I inquired he said that he was just going to watch the slaughter; that "It was on."

As I recall—dimly through the sheet of remembered pain—you beat my ass righteously for 1 hour and 40-some minutes as pay back for those two seconds of humiliation.

The pictures in the article I am linking to ***Stick & Dagger*** were also from sparring with you. You injured me bad enough that you had to treat me like your grandmother for the next month. Also, when sparring with Aaron, he hurt me worse than when he was focused on victory. The point is sparring and fighting overlap in severity depending on the format and the match up.

At the End of Masculine Time

When Chuck and I started we never sparred, but only fought. By 2004 I sparred 20 minutes for every bout I fought. It has gone steadily up from there. I now spar roughly 20 hours for every bout I fight— and I don't get hurt fighting, but in sparring, as we have a lot of time for variables to intrude in sparring.

My goal was to clock as many bouts as I could to determine the injury profile for what I hoped might one day be a professional sport. I began when I was 36 when recovering from a life time of injury, am technically a weakling, have only average athletic ability, and am small. My opponents have averaged half my age and 50 pounds larger. I have fought some of the best stick-fighters in the world and lost almost every one of those bouts in brutal fashion. I trust that makes my record of injuries read alongside my record of combat, a reliably conservative case study for any future governing body for a legitimate unarmored stick-fighting conference to consider.

I hope to make it to 700 bouts with your cruel help Charles. I could care less how many I win. I have already lost over 150 stick fights, and only won 7 out of 21 boxing matches. In stick-fighting terms I've simply become information.

When I get to the end of the road just let me fall.

On 'Escaping the Secular'

Modernity and a View of the Death of Art from the Literary Trenches

The title is inspired by Alex Kurtagic's brilliant introduction to Supernatural Horror in Literature by H.P. Lovecraft.

Last week a fellow writer who works on video game design began asking me questions about the Greek period 750-650 B.C. in support of his latest project. [After checking my notes I amended this to 650-590.] Seeing quickly that I could save this guy a year's research by taking but a portion of two weeks of my time, I wanted to help. Based on the number of online readers that read the ancient combat page I hit on writing a sourcebook and posting it a chapter at a time. I would then be providing free content for our supporters and helping him at the same time.

More importantly I would be generating a companion to the Triumph RPG, which was written in 2012, but due to the fact that I have my faithful sidekick Charles scouring the bars and fitness clubs for nubile virgins upon which I might slack my barbaric thirsts, we are still behind on the project and it would be nice to come up with a sourcebook right out of the gate.

Most importantly, even though such a product as my friend would write would, if successful, be emasculated and debased, I feel I owe it to the ancient warriors who built the society that we call Western Civilization to represent them authentically, hoping that at least an iota of truth might squeak through the Mangina Matrix.

Art As Enterprise

From the beginning my friend, who I will call TNUC, was thrilled that I was helping him, but equally panicked about the prospect of what he had selected as a fairly uninformed random date turning out to be the next big thing in sword and sandals fiction. Below is a progression of our two phone conversations had while I was walking to the market on two different days.

Sensing his paranoia early on about his big idea just being taken away from him like a toddler having his stick of cotton candy snatched by a Goth teen, I disguised the identity and the nature of the project, declaring it a novel. My first inclination was that this man either had no faith in his art, or no faith that art was worth anything in his field of writing.

TNUC/James Dialogue

"I cannot believe you are just throwing this research out there for free after all the work you did. How are you going to make ends meet?"

"Look, I have 26 novels outlined, none of them for this period. Besides, I don't own history. There are also my readers to consider, who like this material and who support the site."

"But with all the writers that come to your site aren't you afraid that they'll just take something you did and remold it and make it theirs?"

"I don't get your concern. I'd be perfectly okay with a contest whereby I and another author write the same subject at the same time. I don't understand fearing other writers—they inspire me."

"Okay James, you are on board; consider yourself a member of the team. You will be on the credits. Do you want to hear the ending?"

"No, I'm just providing research and have no interest in your storyline."

"But we need to discuss the project as we go."

"It's not my project. My part will be over in mere weeks. I am providing you a generic sourcebook that you might make of what you will."

"Okay then, let me ask you, what about possible female characters—a lead. I know it is the most outworn trope in fiction, but if I'm going to sell this there has to be a violent female lead."

"I figured so much considering your market. That is why I selected 650 B.C. as that year Sappho of Lesbos was alive and she is virtually the only name female between the mythic Gods, a queen, and a few fictional characters in plays. Also, if there ever were Amazons, they were around at this period, from 700 to 600." [This statement was incorrect, with Sappho living from about 630 to sometime after 590. Her admirer, Alceus, who was a generation older when he wrote about her beauty, is generally dated at 650, and this date seemingly transposed itself in my mind as her's.]

"Amazons! Are you sure? That could mean bank!"

"Look Amazons were mythic—I'm talking about the cultic basis for the tribal myth. They have been done extensively in fiction for the Classical period, which is totally off base, as they would have been Archaic and possibly late Geometric. I'm giving you the most realistic interpretation in Chapter 5."

"This is marvelous—please, name the lead character. I can't thank you enough. And we have to have regular discussions."

"I will send you the glossary for generating names. I write in a trance and cannot use the phone. As soon as I pick up the phone and have a conversation, the writing day is done. There will not be discussions. I'm writing you a book."

TNUC/James Emails

"The online sources say the Amazons were gone by 700 B.C."

"The online sources are not reliable. There were no Amazons. They were only a possibility between 700 and perhaps 550."

"Okay, I trust you. You can't publish anything pertaining to my storyline."

"That is why I don't know the storyline—did not want to know. I am providing a distillation of available data for the period and locale, for you and my readers."

"You must not publish anything on [names five mythic figures] or the period I am writing in until this project is done. Do not post anything that could be used as research by another writer before running it by me."

The End of Art

So there we stand; another soul that sold itself to the God of Things; a soul that demands I ride to hell with it on the back of its stillborn god in pursuit of an increased share of some thief's debased promise.

So, I close here, letting my readers know that 14 days of my work free of charge, is not enough for a priest of the God of Things, for he must own my soul too, must make claim to a mean-spirited attempt to hide what has been from others so that he might have the flavor of the week on his particular cotton candy stick, and might be envied by the other children that now piss in a sewer for money and call it art.

I have decided to illuminate a tiny corner of the past in a certain light for the interest and enjoyment of those who care. I have no desire to help a sell-out for whom the suffering of countless souls and the triumph of a handful over a hundred year period is nothing but a quarter to be slid into a media approval slot machine.

TNUC did do me a favor, sparking an interest in something I had worked over for years and had set aside.

So TNUC, I owe you an inspirational debt—and fuck you! Don't ever tell me what I can publish. I'd murder your masters for saying that to me. Say it to my face at your peril.

Amazons go up today, as promised.

Comments

fatmanjudo   January 12, 2015 2:43 PM EST

Joy in the pursuit,

A virgin on a bar stool,

Illumination.

fatmanjudo   January 8, 2015 8:33 PM EST

"Nubile virgins" from bars and fitness clubs? Don

Quixote sends sancho panza. Might as well be searching for a unicorn. You'll never finish.

 **responds:** January 9, 2015 3:40 PM EST

It is supposed to be a difficult quest after all. As his mentor the development of Charles' character is my primary concern, with the sacrifice of my sensibility upon finding out that the improbably skilled lady he acquired for me was not as pure as advertised, being the cruel price I must pay.

'Are The Counter-Currents People Cowards?'

A Man Question from George About Secretive White Dissidents

"The Counter-Current guys are supposed to be coming here to Baltimore to have a meeting but are keeping it secret because of that thing that happened in Illinois **_Militant Devolution_**. I'm not exactly a White Nationalist. But I support them and believe they have a right to meet and not be attacked by a bunch of leftists. You probably think their cowards."

Okay George, if the Counter-Currents publishers came to Baltimore I'd be thrilled to meet them, even though I fornicate with the occasional Jewess. They are publishers of unpopular views and I am a writer of unpopular views, after all.

Cowardice?

I have charged various White Nationalists with cowardice for various reasons. I am a Counter-Currents reader and I find absolutely no cause for charging that publisher or its authors with cowardice. The only acts of cowardice that, in my unpopular opinion, a publisher can be guilty of, is voluntary self-censorship in the matter of opinion [not taste]. Writers are only judged cowards by this heathen when they use a pen name.

As for your opinion that they have a 'right' to safely meet, I disagree. I do not believe in rights. A right is a privilege that is enforced by a violent third party action. Rights are by definition cowardice as social artifice.

Additionally, people who wish to gather to discuss ideas, and choose to do so in privacy, are showing good tactical sense, and as Jack Donovan amply articulated in The Way of Men **_'The Primitive Math Of Violence'_**, being a man really comes down to thinking and acting tactically, not puffing your chest out and hooting like some bald chimp. So long as they provide for their privacy through their own means—negotiated, won or purchased—and thus achieve this state through might of the body or mind, than they have no need of a 'right.'

As to the dilemma of the Counter-Currents publishers and writers, and other such proto-political groups in the seeking of secure discussion venues, I do have opinions based on my limited experience providing security for others, which I shall put forward in the article, Tactically Speaking: Securing Your Dissident Venue.

Tactically Speaking

Securing Your Dissident Venue

George, an avid online and print reader, who has had occasion to speak with me in person, is very much interested in supporting men's groups, mostly along 'White Nationalist' lines. As a former liberal, and then a reactionary conservative, who has spent time drinking from the Well of Lilith offered up by each of these bankrupt philosophies, he has become a backer of discussion platforms, such as Counter-Currents, Eradic, American Renaissance, American New Right, etc.

From my readings of these online magazines they seem to fall into the 'pre-political' sphere, in other words discussion platforms that may eventually serve as the basis for a political movement, a political movement being an effort to achieve dominance over other men via persuasion, threat, or naked force. George is not a voter and is not power minded. He simply sees himself as a supporter of alternative ideas, and has asked me how such groups of intellectuals might be able to get together for safe and uninterrupted discussion under our increasingly oppressive Left Wing regime.

I will endeavor to offer what I imagine as advice for a lone intellectual who finds himself at the nexus of a web of like-minded souls separated by geography, and increasingly unable to be able to communicate confidentially under the blooming Surveillance State. For such a person who might be called upon to travel from city to city to meet with supporters, what are the dangers he faces and the countermeasures within his modest means?

Know Your Enemies

If you operate in the realm of ideas your enemies include:

1. The State

2. Political factions

3. The news media

4. Educational institutions

5. Ultimately those political factions that eventually grow up around your ideas. There will come a time when the politicians will need to manipulate your thoughts to make themselves' more successful, and at that point you will no longer be needed and your useful contributions to the pre-political thought process will be retained as your legacy as you and your wireframe glasses are shunted off to…

The Best Discussion Venues

1. Private residence in a congested urban area

2. Secluded residence in a rural area

3. An urban bar in which the owner has been paid to close for a private party

4. A funeral home—the best option really

5. Any other venue is stupid.

6. If you have reason to believe people want to stop your discussion than reserving space in an eatery without first informing the owner of the risk is reprehensible and stupid. He might well be willing to provide security. I know a Greek who owns a diner and counts his money next to the front door at a booth with a 1911 .45 auto on his lap. Ethnic business owners are generally very protective of their turf.

7. Don't have your talk on a Friday or Saturday night like some yuppie prince, but on a Sunday, Monday or Tuesday when everything will be cheaper and easier.

What You Want in a Security Team

1. You do not want a believer in your work, your cause, a zealot, etc. The last thing you want is a

member of your supporting network who offers to fight for you. That guy has masculinity issues.

2. You do not want criminals, but straight actors who will provide criminal levels of practical discretion. Again, your worst security risk is a security team member who is emotionally or ideologically involved or vested. You need a man loyal to you or his profession.

3. A lead who understands how to select and defend the venue: minimal window frontage, diverse neighborhood [which is probably against your factional sympathies but is most easily defended], a narrow front door, a covered egress point.

4. Any security work with less than 3 men is highly problematic. If you have been unable to fill the three basic positions are you are best off with the lead.

5. The lead is slightly to moderately larger than you, stays within sight of you at all times, is intelligent and able to assign tasks to other team members. He makes the arrangements and is, in the end, your bullet catcher.

6. The plug is a big cool man who is usually put on a door.

7. The fixer is a roving scout, who is in charge of keeping the plug and the lead briefed as to developing threats, and is the egress specialist, the guy that gets you out the back door. He is also the most violent team member and ideally not large enough to draw attention. For instance he might let the door man know that five left wingers with hammers are headed his way and then either call the cops or hit them from behind depending on the protocols laid down by the lead. This is the only guy that should be hitting anybody. You can't afford for the plug or the lead to be arrested, and he could be replaced with a passive lookout with a cell phone in a pinch. In case you can't tell, this was my job.

8. As a low profile client you don't want a wall of meat making you look like a mafia don. You want a guy on you that can carry or shield you if necessary, a big mug on the door, and some evil twerp roving the area on the lookout for trouble. Ideally the twerp identifies a developing group—perhaps lefties piling out of a van—and just starts a disturbance that brings cops or attention and the people sent to spoil your little speech never even get to the building.

9. If all you have is a lead he locks the front door—which the venue owner will want secured in any case—and asks someone you trust who is not too interested in your subject to sit across the street with a cell phone to warn him.

10. You will be best served by a bar owner in a high crime area as he already has numerous protocols and possibly auxiliary staff for dealing with the locals who are apt to be much tougher than any interlopers and might even serve as a deterrent.

Good luck.

Fear of Strangers

Hate, Xenophobia & Masculinity

Xenophobia is something that we can expect to see more of from White Identified Americans as this nation's slave masters import cheap third world labor in order to increase their slave holdings. The word Xenophobia, literally translated from the ancient Greek, reads, Stranger-fear.

As you, as a man, begin to realize that your lack of willing service to your slave master will simply be nullified by your slave master acquiring more obedient slaves, without a thought of freeing you,

you will find that some of the like-minded defiant will be 'haters' who believe that all non-whites are evil parasites with unique and inbred flaws in their character that are not present in whites. As naïve as this belief seems to people who have lived in mixed race settings, there is another equally irrational belief that pairs with it. This is the notion that the newly arrived slaves in our pen are on the side of the masters; nothing but their foot soldiers with no hopes, dreams, hates or regrets of their own. This is what any slave master wants, division between those he is exploiting.

When I was a young man such notions of white pride were most often expressed as street level violence by small groups of skinheads against colored women and children and lone men. These attacks were rarely punished and never effective at deterring 'inferior' races from settling in the exclusionary area.

A generation later we have laws in place designed to punish members of the majority group [which is still white despite dark fantasies to the contrary] from doing violence against blacks and other privileged groups. Now, even if defending against blacks—and even if a law officer—prosecution and persecution is likely. You whites are no longer your masters' favorite type of slave. This has placed the awesome fear inspired by the state machine that once terrorized Native Americans and blacks as a threat to whites. The result is fear of other races and the notion that a white enclave should stand somewhere in this land as a kind of militarized reservation for white refugees.

I pity these white men who so doubt themselves that they ascribe superhuman qualities to members of the races they loathe. Despite examples of MMA and boxing matches in which white men tend to dominate blacks our racist mythology persists that a white man without a gun is helpless against a black, and that since the government is against citizens having guns it needs to be changed, to what I do not know.

Once you have been contacted by such activists, or stumble upon them in the martial arts school or work place as I have, they will attempt to emasculate you according to a certain process. The irony is that although these White Nationalist types seek out fighting men as the Aryan Nation once sought out skin heads and the mafia once sought out Irish tough guys, to provide muscle, they will inevitably subject you to the following emasculating agenda:

At the End of Masculine Time

1. Whites are physically inferior to other races and therefore need superior technology, which therefore requires political action to insure survival.

2. Despite uncounted heroic defenses, conquests and last stands by tiny outnumbered and often outgunned white soldiers around the world, that a white man cannot defend himself against other races if he is outnumbered.

3. To prevent the above unwinnable battles—for you cannot fight white man—you must treat unfairly with other races on an individual basis. Therefore, since all other races seek with vast hive minds to do away with the white race you must treat every member of another race with extreme dishonor, regarding him as a criminal, a thief, a liar, thereby destroying your own code of honor, which is the behavioral pillar of the warrior ethic, and in the end what we fall back on when we fight.

4. Since this is believed to be a genetic battle and that morality derives directly from genetics with negligible environmental or learned influence any negative behavior on the part of your white brothers is to be overlooked as they are on your side right or wrong. Throwing your support behind

criminals will further erode your honor and hence your masculine character.

5. Blind support of the collectivist tribal ethics that such groups promote will result in your enslavement and total emasculation. Eventually you will be paying protection money to someone.

6. Savvy organizers will use female agents to attract warrior types to their cause. Before you go down that road read Samson and the Philistines from the Book of Judges, for an example of exactly what fearful tribes do to the warriors they 'coax' by way of the machinations of the sweet sex.

A Positive Masculine Alliance

In the interest of you masculinity—which is your very identity as a human and the basis for your status as a warrior—consider the following keys to joining a cause that will be less likely to erode your honor. Keep in mind that modern militaries, criminal gangs and police forces are based on the negation of individual honor in favor of the primacy of collective honor.

At the End of Masculine Time

1. Only accept the proposal of men who approach you as men. A man who sends a woman is not a man, least of all honorable.

2. Do not submit, but join, or ally.

3. A handshake or similar bond is preferable to a written contract, just like punching me is more masculine than writing about it.

4. The alliance shall not be based on fear.

5. The alliance shall be based on shared values.

6. The alliance is strongest when there is a shared hate.

7. Ideally that which is hated is counter to your shared values.

There are a lot more things to ponder but I consider the above points to be crucial and basic to the question of lending your strength to others. Overall, if a warrior is motivated by fear of anything other than failure he is the weaker for it. And fear of strangers is simply stupid, as it is necessarily based on weak intelligence.

At the End of Masculine Time

www.ingramcontent.com/pod-product-compliance
Lightning Source LLC
Chambersburg PA
CBHW070536290526
45790CB00002B/527